Around Bude and Strat

by

JOAN RENDELL

Best wishes,
Joan Rendell.

Bossiney Books

For Zeus, who loved above all walking beside
the canal at Bude.

First published in 1985 by Bossiney Books,
St Teath, Bodmin, Cornwall.
Designed, printed and bound by A. Wheaton & Co. Ltd., Exeter.
© Joan Rendell 1985
ISBN 0 906456 94 0

About the Author – and the Book

Joan Rendell is one of Bossiney's most prolific authors. This is her seventh title for the Cornish cottage publishers, and she has contributed to the widely acclaimed *The Cornish Year Book*.

She made her debut for Bossiney in 1979 with *Along the Bude Canal* following it with such diverse titles as *Hawker Country*, *Lundy*, *Gateway to Cornwall*, *Cornish Churches*, and, more recently, *North Cornwall in the Old Days*.

The daughter of a St Austell father and a Helston mother, Joan Rendell has travelled extensively: to every country in Europe – except Iceland – to the Middle East, North Africa and the Americas. She is a frequent lecturer and contributes to a variety of publications, including *This England* and *Cornish Life*. Her authorship encompasses such contrasting works as books on Matchbox Labels and Country Crafts, Flower Arrangements and Corn Dollies. Her passion for matchbox labels began at the age of eight, and her collection, now totalling 205,000, is one of the largest in the world.

In September, 1980, Joan Rendell was initiated as a Bard of the Cornish Gorseth, taking the name of *Scryfer Weryn* – Writer of Werrington. She lives in the Parish of Werrington, through which the Bude Canal once flowed.

In 1958 she was awarded the MBE and in 1977 the Queen's Silver Jubilee Medal.

In this, her latest Bossiney title, Joan Rendell explores Bude and Stratton and the Bude Canal which she describes as 'one of the greatest although much underestimated engineering projects of its time . . .'

The text, reinforced by photographs ancient and modern, enables us to go back in mood and time to a much loved area of North Cornwall.

Personalities, like R.S. Hawker, the giant Anthony Payne, Sir Goldsworthy Gurney, and Samuel Seccombe, people the pages. Fun and frolic, the building of the Canal, the birth of Bude as a resort and a tour around Stratton are only some of the ingredients that will bring back nostalgic memories for the older generation – and open the eyes of the younger.

3

BUDE – THE BIRTH OF A RESORT

Bude and Stratton go naturally together – like roast beef and Yorkshire pudding or, more appropriately, strawberries and Cornish cream.

Sir John Betjeman called Stratton 'the county town of northernmost Cornwall, on a Roman road to

'It was at the end of the nineteenth century that Bude, as we know it today, began to emerge.'

Cornwall, the mother of Bude . . .' So first let us go to Bude. Sir John went there too. '. . . the least rowdy modern seaside town in Cornwall,' he reflected, 'a counterpart to Devon's Sidmouth.'

It must be quite a traumatic experience – in one century merely just a village in the Hundred of Stratton, in the next a fast-growing and popular resort. But that is just what happened to Bude.

In the seventeenth century and well into the eighteenth and even nineteenth it was no more than

the usual fishing village, the straggle of fishermen's cottages, a manor house and a tide mill, an area more or less cut off from the rest of Cornwall, even of England.

The famous Arundel- or Arundell-family held sway there, just as in other parts of Cornwall. These days it is often difficult to visualise the power and authority which great families wielded in the past but in the early days they owned not only land but people and their way of life as well, in the sense that everything revolved around them and their estates and properties.

The Arundels and the Grenvilles of Stowe owned most of the land around Bude, or Bede Haven as it was then, which of course meant all the properties on it as well. It was said that the River Neet marked the boundary between Arundel and Grenville land and woe betide one family's tenants trying to encroach on the land of the other's.

The Arundel stone in the wall of Leven Cottages, Bude.

In the nineteenth century the Arundel land came into the possession of the Acland family and Sir Thomas Acland was largely responsible for the development of Bude. Acland was a name also prominently linked with the Bude Canal and buildings on Sir Thomas Dyke Acland's private wharf on the canal stand to this day. By that time, too, Lords Clinton and Carteret also owned land in the vicinity and the face of Bude was very much changed from when Richard Carew surveyed it in the seventeenth century.

It was at the end of the nineteenth century that Bude, as we know it today, began to emerge. At that time one of the most popular periodicals in the county was *The Cornish Magazine*, edited by A.T. – later Sir Arthur – Quiller-Couch. In 1899 the magazine ran a feature on 'How to Develop Cornwall as a Holiday Resort' and the response it evoked both flattered and insulted some places in Cornwall but none more outspokenly than that levelled at Bude by a Miss J.H. Findlater – 'not a native of Cornwall' she hastened to point out – which was published in *The Cornish Magazine*.

'Bude is a place with many natural advantages: sands, cliffs, downs, a river', she wrote, 'yet by a promiscuous and unrestrained building it has been turned into a perfect eyesore.' Even worse was to come. Miss Findlater continues: 'Great rows of cheaply run up lodging houses stand in tiers on the cliff side and every abomination of the jerry builder is to be seen here to the greatest advantage.'

Incidentally, what has happened to all those so called jerry built edifices now? Miss Findlater proved, however, to be not a very good prophet; perhaps it was wishful thinking that caused her to pen: 'Doubtless Bude will have its day and cease to be fashionable and another Bude, worse than the first, will rise on

Canal and river meet the Atlantic at Bude.

The Falcon Hotel, Bude, in coaching days.

the now untouched wildness of the splendid western shores; or perhaps now that the railway has reached so near to it, even dear Marhamchurch will be "discovered", "developed" and destroyed.'

One wonders what Miss Findlater would think if she could return to Bude today or even to Marhamchurch. True the latter has grown and not always with the type of 'development' which is suited to Cornish villages but it is certainly not quite so horrific as Miss Findlater envisaged.

By the mid nineteenth century Bude was already coming into its own as a resort and the discerning traveller in need of rest and relaxation was fast discovering it. *An Illustrated Itinerary of the County of Cornwall* published in 1853 says, 'Bude is a bathing place, where retirement and quiet may be found in a degree seldom experienced in the anomalous towns generally so styled.' Bully for Bude!

The same volume also graciously declares, 'Bude may have some claim to attention. The western

The coming of the railway made a great difference to Bude, for not only did it enable more visitors to come to the resort, but it also speeded up the delivery of newspapers.

Two earlier views of Bude: Above, Queen's Street.
Right, alongside the River Neet.

breezes come in pure from the Atlantic and the pestilent east wind is unfelt, the port being sheltered by lofty hills.' The writers of modern guides to the town might bear those points in mind when 'selling' the resort to up-country holidaymakers.

These days we tend to regard Bude as the 'parent' town with Stratton something of a 'suburb' or adjoining and smaller town, but in fact the reverse is the case. An amusing account of this state of affairs was given by a writer in the *Illustrated Itinerary* of the mid eighteen hundreds. He claims it illustrates what he calls 'the pretension in Bude' at that time.

Summoning a waitress in the hotel where he was staying he asked for hot water because there was

none in the teapot and he asked for it to be brought in a tea-kettle, only to be told by the waitress – 'with a slight flourish of the head' – 'The urn is coming Sir; we don't use tea-kettles like the Stratton people.' The writer notes 'the incipient effort to be exclusive' while at the same time adding that 'Stratton was an ancient town when Bude was a sand-bank'. He goes on: ' "They do that at Stratton" may in future serve as a gibe at anything done out of the mode.' The sort of thing that we can chuckle at today but deadly serious in its time.

The Bude and Stratton area has actually been settled since at least the Bronze Age. There are barrows on Maer Down and other elevated sites but

Building the wall in 1877 along Bude's 'prom'.

none have yielded any outstanding treasures.

Bude's 'prom' does not overlook the sea; it can roughly be described as the gently curving pavement which follows the line of the River Neet from Nanny Moore's Bridge to Bencoolen Bridge. Here one begins to enter the 'suburbs' which inconspicuously merge into Stratton by way of modern 'ribbon development'.

An old photograph of 1877 shows the wall being built along this attractive stretch of road. Prior to that the land simply sloped gently to the river. There was no pavement, just a rough road running in front of

dwelling houses, an inn and a warehouse, where there are now shops, an arcade and hotels. A building is shown right in the middle of what is now The Triangle; where a bank stands today on the corner was Bude Hotel with its name painted in huge letters across the façade and tiny cottages stood where there are now shops. In the photograph there is not much evidence of that jerry building which so upset the redoubtable Miss Findlater twenty years later.

The River Neet flows into the sea and is crossed by what is now known as Nanny Moore's Bridge, taking

Nanny Moore's Bridge and Leven Cottages at Bude in 1900. 'The mill here was a tide mill, dependent for its operation on the rise and fall of the tide.'

its name from a widow called Moore who lived in the old millhouse in the nineteenth century and who was described as a 'dipper'. Just what her function was in that respect seems to have been lost in the mists of time but 'dipper' was once used as a contemptuous term for the Baptists, so Mrs Moore's title might have referred to her religious beliefs. The mill there was a tide mill, dependent for its operation on the rise and fall of the tide.

Corn mills were all tied in with Bude's importance as a port in days gone by. *The Universal British Directory of 1791* speaks of considerable trade being carried on: exporting corn, particularly oats, to different parts of the kingdom and vast quantities of bark to Ireland for tanning and importing coals and salt from Wales and Bristol respectively.

The fishing industry was also important in Bude's early days and some strange happenings occurred from time to time. For instance, on the Tuesday and Wednesday evenings of the first week in September

Scene at the well at the bottom of Lansdowne Road – the town's water supply in the nineteenth century – after the Great Blizzard.

1856 what was described at the time as 'a very unusual occurrence' took place. The coming tide on those days brought into the harbour myriads of sprats and shads. These were carted away from the beach by the donkey-load and sold in the town and neighbouring villages at from fourpence to sixpence (old money) per hundred.

Although a nineteenth-century writer described Bude as not suffering an east wind, conditions were not and still are not always balmy, especially in the winter months. A newspaper report of 31 December 1874 records that 'at Bude on Wednesday the snow-storm was most severe. The roads away from the coast on towards the moors are impassable and the mails were seven hours behind their time'. Well, there you are, but it *did* say 'away from the coast', so perhaps Bude itself didn't suffer so badly after all and enjoyed those western breezes instead.

An interesting picture of Bude at the turn of the century has emerged from a report in the *Cornish & Devon Post* dated 28 October 1922 which gives details of a lecture given by Mrs A. Saunders on the subject of 'Bude in the Olden Days'. In her lecture Mrs Saunders revealed that there was at one time a public house near Nanny Moore's Bridge, known as 'The Jolly Sailor'. No trace of that remains today.

Mrs Saunders recalled that before the present breakwater was constructed there was a less durable structure but one which she described as 'by far the more beautiful of the two', being built of massive stones, standing twenty feet high with a promenade ten feet wide ending in a pier head. Apparently it did

Mr Thomas Yeo, Bude Town Crier, in 1912.

not last for long despite its attractive appearance and once it was breached it took only two tides to destroy it. The chairman at that meeting was a Mr F. Jeffery, a descendant of Nanny Moore, who gave her name to the bridge, and he recalled that in 1822 there were only seven houses in Bude, most of them being near Nanny Moore's Bridge.

Mrs Saunders spoke of something which seems very quaint today – the time when there was a men's beach and a women's beach and each sex kept very carefully to its own domain, 'it being a terrible thing for a man to visit the ladies' beach and vice versa'! Incidentally, Bude was always famous for its fine sea bathing, even long before it became an acknowledged seaside resort.

Mrs Saunders called Bude in the olden days 'a terrible place, both for smuggling and wrecking' and she remembered personal stories about some of the many wrecks on this coast. She quoted the case of the *Eliza*, loaded with general cargo which included some beautiful sheeting, 'some of which, by some mysterious manner, found its way into many of the houses in the locality'. This gave rise to a couplet which originated in the town: 'The *Eliza* of Liverpool came ashore, To feed the hungry and clothe the poor.'

What a wealth of human interest stories older people were able to tell about parts of Cornwall which at that time were virtually 'off the map' as far as visitors from across the Tamar were concerned.

'Bude is a bathing place, where retirement and quiet may be found . . .'

Right: Bude breakwater photographed in 1905 by Herbert Hughes. A mining engineer, Hughes toured Cornwall every year with J.C. Burrow and Herbert Thomas from, it is thought, 1897 up to the First World War.

DOWN TO THE SEA

Bude is dominated by the sea. Not unexpected for a seaside town but somehow in Bude the presence of the sea on its doorstep seems to infiltrate, even more than in other places, the life of the town and the town itself.

The roar of the sea can be heard from several miles away when the wind is in the north; nearer to the actual coastline its constant roar is a permanent background noise but no one complains that it is 'noise pollution' or calls in the environmental health department! It does, in fact, constitute one of the charms of Bude and some older residents say that they could never live anywhere away from the sound of waves pounding on the rocks.

That famous chronicler, Richard Carew, whose *Survey of Cornwall* was dated 1602, described Bude as 'an open sandy bay, in whose mouth riseth a little hill, by every sea flood made an island and theron a decayed chapel'. He goes on to say, 'it spareth road only to such small shipping as bring their tide with them, leaving them dry when the ebbeth carried away the salt water' – a graphic if somewhat uninviting description!

Chapel Rock, the 'little hill', is still a feature but the building of the breakwater for the construction of the canal meant that it was no longer an island as in Carew's day.

Bude is dominated by the sea. When the breakwater was built, Chapel Rock was no longer an island.

The Ceres – Bude –   Joan Moodge

It is difficult to picture Bude as a busy port filled with the wooden hulled ketches which were the mainstay of the Cornish coasting trade, plus the occasional smacks and schooners which also used the port. One of these vessels has gone down in history and is remembered by many people even today. The ketch *Ceres* was as much a part of Bude as the name of the town itself. She was built at Salcombe, Devon, in 1811 and had an adventurous history in her early days, being involved among other things in carrying stores in the Peninsular War. She was taken to Bude in 1826 and bought in 1852 by one of the best known names of those times in the town, Henry Petherick, and she remained Petherick property through four generations.

Ceres was a sailing ketch but in 1912 she was fitted with a small auxiliary engine to give her a little more potential. During World War I she miraculously steered clear of German submarines and continued her peaceful plodding way, bringing all manner of cargoes into Bude from other ports around the British Isles. She weathered many a storm which claimed lesser vessels and she remained a fully rigged sailing ketch to the end of her days, a never-to-be-missed attraction for anyone paying a visit to Bude. As a small child, taken from Launceston to Bude on the bus for a day's outing, my first request was always 'Let's go to see if *Ceres* is in' and I loved that old vessel with a child's uninhibited passion.

When news came of her final sinking in 1936 I cried quarts of bitter tears and to this day I never walk along by her former berth without whispering to her a secret 'rest in peace' as her remains lie off one of the most treacherous stretches of the North Devon coast. In 1936 she sprang a leak whilst rounding Baggy Point: her Captain Jeffrey and his crew were rescued

The sailing ketch Ceres, *'a truly remarkable old lady' and well known in Bude. At that time she was the oldest ship on Lloyd's Register, having completed 125 years of service. Captured on canvas by Joan Madge (left).*

by Appledore lifeboat but despite the most strenuous efforts nothing could be done to save her.

Those who only knew Bude since the demise of *Ceres* have missed a great experience in their lives. Incidentally, she was the oldest vessel on the British Register of Shipping and bore the wonderful record of having completed one hundred and twenty five years of unstinting service without the loss of a single member of her crews. She was truly a remarkable 'old lady', the like of which will never be seen again.

Ceres was refitted at Stapleton's Shipyard, another Bude institution, and the maintenance of these old 'wooden walls' was no job for weaklings or the workshy. Stapleton's yard actually lengthened *Ceres* in 1865 to enable her to carry more cargo and this called for very careful calculation, since ships using

Bude harbour have always been restricted in size on account of the length and width of the sea lock constructed for the canal.

The skill of the old sea captains in getting their vessels through this narrow entrance with sometimes only inches to spare on either side is mirrored today by the skill of the coach drivers edging their huge vehicles into seemingly far too narrow spaces in the carparks. Bude's trade today comes by road instead of sea.

In 1837 King William IV presented Bude with its first lifeboat, largely at the request of the famous vicar of Morwenstow, the Reverend R.S. Hawker. The previous year Mr Hawker had started a fund to provide a lifeboat for Bude, making the first donation, of one pound, himself, a donation probably equivalent to about twenty five pounds today. His father and brother each subscribed ten shillings but the fund was slow in growing and so Mr Hawker wrote the king one of the begging letters which he was so good at composing, and once again he achieved success and Bude got its lifeboat.

In 1866 the first of the RNLI's lifeboats for Bude arrived and was stationed there for many years. Now Bude has no full-size lifeboat because trade by sea into the port has declined to almost nil but there is an RNLI inshore rescue boat which performs sterling service and is manned by local volunteers.

However, the first lifeboat was not an unmitigated success. According to contemporary reports it was imperfectly constructed and this was illustrated in a sad tragedy soon after the boat arrived.

'It is difficult to picture Bude as a busy port filled with the wooden-hulled ketches which were the mainstay of the Cornish coasting trade . . .'

Masts in the canal basin below the Falcon Hotel.

On an October day in 1845 the usual lifeboat exercise was scheduled to take place and according to a newspaper report of the time, 'the whole village turned out to keep the afternoon as a holiday. To see the practice was a new amusement for the boat had only recently been put on the station.'

All went well as the boat pulled away with twelve men manning the oars and another man steering. However, at the narrow entrance to the harbour a freak current appeared to take the boat and it was

26

turned broadside on. The men got confused, a couple of waves followed one another more quickly than usual and the boat upset, floating bottom upwards.

Two men scrambled out and climbed on to the keel and the boat slowly drifted towards land and grounded, whereupon many eager hands pulled her up. Nine men were still underneath but they had been saved by two large holes in the bottom of the boat, a part of the 'imperfect construction'. Tragically two men of the thirteen on board were drowned in

'Bude has been the scene of many wrecks . . .' – the town had its first lifeboat in 1837.

the incident and were never found, although the search went on for the rest of the day and through the night, people with lanterns searching among the rocks in the hope of recovering the bodies after the tide went down.

Something which puzzles many visitors to Bude is the Half Tide Cross. This iron cross rising out of the water at the point of a rock ledge is a dramatic looking feature and to the uninitiated it quite naturally conjures up visions of a grave, a shipwreck and all sorts of grisly possibilities.

However, it represents nothing so sensational. Tides have always proved a problem for shipping at Bude. Storms and gales make entry to the harbour a near impossibility and ships could enter or leave the

harbour only during a few hours each day because of the vagaries of the tides.

In the early days there were no Admiralty tide tables and forecasting the tides was a tricky business calling for much skill and know-how. The first tide tables were not printed until 1843 and prior to that Sir Thomas Acland's son Arthur in conjunction with the then harbourmaster, a Mr Gorman, calculated times and depths of water at the Bude sea lock, as an aid to mariners.

It was about that period that the Half Tide Cross came into being. Standing as it does at the end of Coach Rock, it indicates that when the water is level with the arm of the cross the tide is half way between high and low. It proved an invaluable guide in days

Bude's first beach patrolman was Mr George Henry Johnson, pictured here on duty in 1912. He also took visitors out fishing and for boat trips (left).

gone by and is even now carefully observed by the skippers of small craft wishing to enter the harbour. In 1861 Mr Arthur Mills, who lived at Efford Down, was so impressed with the functions of the Half Tide Cross that he was moved to write a six verse poem in honour of it. Some typical lines read:

And half thy daily course is run
That God appointed unto thee
O busy, never resting sea,
When first thy glittering wavelets toss
Their foam around that lowly cross.

Mr Mills lived in a picturesque red-brick mansion standing in its own grounds at Efford Down so he was in a unique position to witness the difficulties of all sea traffic in and out of the harbour.

Over the years Bude has been the scene of many wrecks; possibly no-one will ever know just how many because a lot must have occurred before records were kept. Some of the wrecks have become famous, have gone down in history and have been written about and spoken about on many occasions.

Just such a one was the wreck of the 1,415 ton *Bencoolen* on 21 October 1862 when she was en route from Liverpool to Bombay with general cargo. This ship gave its name to Bencoolen Bridge in Bude and in the churchyard the ship's figurehead was erected beside the memorial stone which tells us that 'Here lie deposited the remains of the Chief Mate and 13 seamen, a portion of the crew of the *Bencoolen* which was wrecked at the entrance to this harbour, Oct. 21st

1862'. Actually there were no less than three wrecks at Bude in that autumn of 1862.

Not all of the wrecks claimed lives although some of them were very spectacular and the circumstances were sometimes most extraordinary. An example of this in February 1904 also illustrates the vicious weather to which Bude has been subjected at times in the past. After a tremendous winter storm in that February the inner lock gates were totally destroyed and this caused the canal to empty, leaving the tide a free flow to work further havoc on the sides of the cutting. Lying moored inside the gates on the Tuesday morning of 1 February were the vessels *Wild Pigeon* and *Jessie*, both waiting ready for sea. When the gates burst open *Wild Pigeon* glided swiftly out into the harbour and into the breakers beyond, the tremendous seas finally driving the ketch on to the rocks under the Summerleaze – then spelt Summer-lease – side of the harbour.

The three men on board saved their lives by jumping on to the canal bank and so the ketch was unmanned when she was swept into the harbour and on to the rocks. Her sails and spars were salvaged the same day but she could not be saved from becoming a total wreck. At the same time the other ship, *Jessie*, was caused to lie athwart the canal and a contemporary newspaper report claimed that the shipping trade would be crippled for some time to come by the serious mishap.

In that storm which ripped away the inner lock gates the effect of the ground sea on the breakwater was devastating; half of what was known as the

Left: The camera of Herbert Hughes captures in 1913 the folded rock strata so familiar along this North Cornish coast.

Waterloo portion of the breakwater was wrecked, destroying the protection to the sea caves belonging to Sir T.D. Acland which was gutted.

On Tuesday, 23 August 1904 crowds gathered to see a demonstration by the lifeboat *Elizabeth Moore Garden* and her crew and two days later the same people were afforded an opportunity of seeing the actual work of saving life at a wreck. On that Thursday afternoon the firing of the gun and rocket to summon the lifeboat crew brought hundreds of people to the cliffs to see what was happening and the sight that met their eyes was the schooner *Crystal Spring* stranded under Maer High Cliffs, only a short distance from the shore and in moderate weather with little sea.

She had been on her way from Liverpool to Bude with a hundred tons of coal. She had gone ashore at half flood and was manned by only two men. The Bude Rocket Brigade saved the men by means of the rocket line, hauling them through the surf. The ship was already breaking up so that neither of the men could get properly into the breeches.

The vessel became a total wreck and on Saturday, 3 September she was sold by auction, the prices realised seeming completely absurd today. Petherick Bros. purchased the hull and spars for ten guineas and the boat for nine shillings. The coal washed out of the hull on to the beach was disposed of for sixpence, the rudder made one shilling and six pence, the steering wheel fourteen shillings, the name board ninepence and the anchors seven shillings and one pound respectively.

Right: The end of Bude breakwater taken in 1913, where the sea's relentless onslaught sculptures the stones.

STRATTON – A FINE AND FAIR TOWN

According to *Lake's Parochial History*, that 'bible' for all students of Cornish history, Stratton takes its name from the Roman road or street near which it stands, such towns being called street-towns or strettons. Other historians have disputed this saying there is no evidence that the Romans ever got as far west as Stratton. So the question remains open to this day.

Today it is a charming place, still retaining some beautiful thatched cottages and with little alleys and courtyards which have hardly changed in centuries – truly somewhere worth exploring.

At the turn of the present century a Mr Arthur Norway, writing about Stratton in a book entitled *Highways and Byways of Devon and Cornwall* says of it: '. . . nowhere in Cornwall are the cottages more picturesque, the streets more narrow or more obviously ancient.' However, in 1830 Pigot's *Directory* was not so enchanted and described the town as 'an inconsiderable place seated in a low and cold country; the land has, however, been improved rather of late years from draining and its general aspect has assumed a more verdant and cheering appearance.' How gracious of the directory compiler to upgrade the town in such a way!

Unfortunately it does seem that Stratton must have been a rather inhospitable place in days gone by because Richard Carew, in his sixteenth-century *Survey of Cornwall* said of it: '. . . memorable matter to

A view of Stratton taken before the First World War.

Stratton in 'primitive' style by an unknown artist.

report thereof, I find not any' and he couldn't have been much briefer and to the point!

That description could certainly not apply to the town now, clustered as it is around its fine parish church, where the father of the famous Reverend R.S. Hawker of Morwenstow was once vicar and where Robert Stephen Hawker lived as a boy.

The manor of Stratton was recorded in the Domesday Book and the first indication that a Norman church existed there came to light when a stone carved with the figures MCLI (1151) was discovered during restoration of the church in 1888. Also the font

is Norman and so is a fragment of a holy water stoup in the south porch.

The famous Sir Ralph de Blanchminster, who did so much for the area, in his will dated 1348 bequeathed 'to the fabric of one aisle of the church of St Andrew of Stratton on the North side ten marks'. He continues, 'I bequeath all the timber competent and sufficient to the same fabric . . .' Thus was built the north aisle.

A mutilated effigy of what is believed to be Sir Ralph is in a window embrasure in the north wall and the Reverend R.S. Hawker of Morwenstow immortalised him in a romantic poem. In fairly recent years the identity of the effigy has been called into question by some historians but as long ago as 1753 an account of the parish by one Reverend Anthony Moore – a document now in the Morrab Library at Penzance – states that the effigy is that of Rodolphus de Albo Monasterio who 'in ancient times had a good country seat and mansion house in this parish called by the name of the Manor of Benomy'.

There is an interesting and little known connection between Stratton and the Bude Canal. It is said that at the time of King John the tide came up to the junction of the River Neete or Strat – Neete being the old Cornish genetic term for a stream – with its tributary just below the town. When the Bude Canal was being constructed anchors dating from Tudor times were excavated at Rodd's Bridge, about one and a half miles further down river, suggesting that quite large ships of that period had used it as an anchorage.

What happened to those anchors no-one knows today. They really should have been preserved in Stratton because the town was very closely connected with the Bude Canal in that it was the centre for the payment of wages to employees of the canal and from which supplies were distributed. The payment and

Stratton Church today and the memorial to the men of the town who gave their lives in the Great War. Left: Stratton Church as it was around 1900.

Late nineteenth-century glimpse inside Stratton Church.

distribution took place on market day in the town and the local inns benefitted considerably on 'wages day'!

Incidentally, the long defunct Pannier Market at Stratton was at one time a focal point for the people living in the countryside for miles around. They came to the market with their produce and they set up their 'stannins' whether they were prosperous farmers' wives with a great deal of poultry and dairy produce to sell or the wife of a poor labourer trying to raise a few coppers from the sale of the snipe which her husband had shot on the marshes.

Coppers were literally all that much of the produce fetched in days gone by; for instance, on Tuesday 29 December 1904 prices realised were: butter 1s. 2d. to 1s. 3d. a pound, eggs 10-12 for 1s., chicken 5s. to 6s. *a couple*, partridges 3s. a brace, snipe 8d. and widgeon

8d. Even allowing for money being worth a great deal more in those days no one could be expected to make a fortune from those sort of prices. In those days it was very true that living in the country was cheap.

A stroll through Stratton can be a delightful experience, gently guiding one back through time as various ancient features of the town are revealed. Opposite the church lychgate stands Church Cottage, a building with wonderful beams and many odd nooks and crannies which is worthy of far more than just a passing glance. It was at one time a double tenement and had an outside staircase leading to the upper floor.

There are records to show that the stairway was a bone of contention during the reign of Henry VIII, when St Andrew's Fair included a market held in the

39

A more leisurely age in Stratton.

square outside the church and Church Cottage. The stall holders complained bitterly that the staircase encroached on to six or seven feet of the square which should have been utilised for the setting up of stalls, whereas those living in Church Cottage protested that the market stalls interfered with access to their staircase and thus entry to their homes. Unfortunately there is no documentary evidence to tell us how the almost insurmountable problem was finally solved.

Later Church Cottage was used by the churchwardens who ran a fund raising project there, brewing beer which was consumed on the premises, the profit going to the church. At Fair times the building was let to merchants to accommodate themselves and their goods and also to gypsies and their dancing bears, the latter not being the most popular of 'lodgers'!

Another interesting old building of a very different sort has recently come into its own again. It is the Old Court House which was restored in 1984 by the Cornwall Buildings Preservation Trust. It is of a much later period than many of the buildings in Stratton, having been erected somewhere between 1810 and 1820 as the seat of justice for the former Stratton Hundred – a hundred having been an administrative division of a county in England, supposed to have originally contained one hundred families or freemen.

It has, however, served many purposes. In order to make it 'pay its way' it was used for several different activities and there still exists an old playbill advertising 'Fashionable Entertainment' by the 'Celebrated and Original Ethiopian Serenaders from St James'. As opposed to that select sort of event a rabbit market was held in the 1900s at the rear of the building under the colonnade – impressive with its cast iron pillars.

In later years the building has been used as a grain

The Old Court House at Stratton restored by the Cornwall Buildings Preservation Trust in 1984.

store, a cycle shop and car dealer's store, whilst the upstairs room, presumably the scene of the theatrical performances of old, was used as the local Working Men's Club and as late as the 1950's the local amateur theatrical society, The Stratton Strollers, gave performances there.

Then along came the Cornwall Buildings Preservation Trust, which buys old buildings worthy of preservation, restores them and converts them to a suitable modern use without destroying their character. So the Trust has splendidly restored the Old Court House and converted it into two semi-detached houses, the occupiers of which will enter both premises through the original elegantly arched doorway. A Cornish slate plaque on the front of the building points it out as a feature of historic interest.

Earlier in the twentieth century the Petty Sessions were held at the Court House on the second Monday in every month at 11 a.m. Some pretty rough justice was meted out in that building; for instance in 1904 William Johnson, a tramp, was committed by the magistrates to ten days hard labour for begging at Rhude Cross and two other men were sent to prison for seven days for the same offence elsewhere in the district.

No-one should visit Stratton without seeing the site of the Battle of Stamford Hill, even though it has little to show today of the scars of history. One of the Civil War guns formerly stood as a monument on the site but it probably went, along with a lot of other irreplaceable 'hardware' in the demand for scrap iron in World War II.

Now the battle site is marked by a rather curious memorial – one of the pinnacles of Poughill Church surmounting a stone arch. The first memorial was placed on the site by Lord Lansdown in 1713 but was said to have soon fallen to pieces. Fixed to it was

an inscribed plaque which was salvaged and set up in the market place in the town. It was later moved and placed on the wall of the Tree Inn, where Sir Bevil Grenville and his officers stayed before the Battle of Stamford Hill, when the building was a manor house.

The tablet is now a prominent feature of that building and the inscription reads: 'In this place the Army of the Rebels under the command of the Earle of Stamford received a signal overthrow by the valour of Sir Bevil Granville (sic) and the Cornish Army on Tuesday the 16th of May 1643.'

In 1971 Bude-Stratton and District Old Cornwall Society donated a new tablet bearing a transcript of

The memorial on the site of the Battle of Stamford Hill consists of a pinnacle from Poughill Church surmounting a stone arch. Left: The tablet on the memorial today.

Sunday morning today in Stratton.

the original text and this metal plate is affixed to the arch which is now part of the memorial. From time to time the Sealed Knot Society re-enacts the Battle of Stamford Hill on the site, as a form of entertainment.

There is a rather grisly story about Stamford Hill and the battle site. At the time of the battle the land on which it was fought had barley growing on it and this was naturally thought to have been trampled underfoot and destroyed. But not at all. The barley revived and the crop was outstandingly fine in both quality and quantity, due, it was assumed to all the human blood which had fertilised the soil. The crop was reputed to have been so fecund that several ears grew on each stalk and some of them were taken around England as a curiosity which people were prepared to pay to view.

Stratton seems to have some propensity towards producing corn freaks. Nearly three hundred years after the Battle of Stamford Hill, in September 1904 to be exact, a Mr L. Gilbert was cutting oats and he put aside one ear of grain as it seemed particularly large. In the evening he counted the grains and found it contained the remarkable number of three hundred and sixty five. But that was nothing to what was to come. A few days later a Mr Butler was also cutting a field of oats and he laid aside a very large ear – that one was found to contain an astonishing five hundred and thirty three grains. Where was *The Guinness Book of Records*?

October trees in Stratton.

Left: Travelling through Stratton in 1984.

STRATTON PEOPLE

Possibly the best known building in Stratton, apart from the church, is the Tree Inn, a former Elizabethan manor house and now a popular hostelry. The dining room ceiling is supported by old ships' timbers and the whole place has loads of 'atmosphere', as should a building around which so many legends have circulated.

Its most famous association is with the so-called Cornish giant, Anthony Payne, steward to Sir Bevil Grenville of Stowe. Payne was reputed to be seven feet four inches tall and was said to have been born in and died at the manor house which is now the Tree Inn, although there are those who dispute that.

During the Civil War Payne accompanied Sir Bevil Grenville on the battlefield and two literary clerics, the Reverend Robert Stephen Hawker of Morwenstow and the Reverend Sabine Baring-Gould of Lewtrenchard, used him as the vehicle for flights of fancy – to which both were prone. Hawker claimed to have discovered a letter of comfort written by Payne

The Tree Inn, Stratton. Note the tablet commemorating the overthrow of the Rebel Army by Sir Bevil Grenville's troops in the Civil War.

A portrait of Sir Bevil Grenville possibly by Van Dyck.

Anthony Payne,The Cornish Giant,
Painted by Sir Godfrey Kneller 1680
by Command of King Charles II.
Presented to the
Royal Institution of Cornwall.
By Sir Robert Harvey.

to Sir Bevil Grenville's widow after Sir Bevil's death in the Battle of Lansdown, near Bath, but authenticated research has since shown that Payne was illiterate and could pen no more than a cross to signify his name.

What is, however, believed to be true is that Payne was a very compassionate man, a real gentle giant, and that while burying the dead after the Battle of Stamford Hill at Stratton, he was about to lower one body into a grave when the man stirred and Payne is said to have taken him back to his (Payne's) cottage, where the giant's wife tended his wounds and the man survived.

The most popular Tree Inn legend is that Payne died in the building and was so big that it was impossible to take his body down the staircase so his coffin was lowered through the dining-room ceiling. However, one modern-day scholar believes that Payne did not die at the Tree Inn but in his own cottage and claims to have by diligent research discovered the approximate spot where the cottage stood.

The full details of that research have not yet, however, been published. What is known for fact is that in the Burial Register of St Andrew's Church, Stratton, the following entries are recorded: 'Burials – Sibella, wife of Anthony Payne 9th July 1691. Anthony Payne 13th July 1691'. Strange that they should die within a week of each other; could it have been plague that carried them off? Stratton was notorious at that time for being a poor and unhealthy town, very different indeed from today.

We shall never know the answer: their burial places

Portrait of Anthony Payne by Kneller – Payne is said to have died in the Tree Inn (right).

Left: The Drangett leading to Gibraltar Square in Stratton. Right: Gibraltar House, former home of Sergeant Robert Smith. Note the two plaques inscribed 'R.S. GIBR. 1785' and '12th Regt. of Foot'. The entrance to the Drangett is on the left.

are not known. During the work on the underpinning of the wall of the south aisle of the church in the nineteenth century a huge lead coffin was uncovered and found to contain the bones of an enormous man but these crumbled to dust when exposed to the air and what could be salvaged of the remains was re-interred. No record was kept of the spot and there is no sign to mark it, so the information has been lost for ever. Incidentally, Anthony Payne was reputed to have weighed over four hundred and fifty pounds but was said by an early writer to have 'not been fat and corpulent'.

When Payne was serving as a halberdier of the guns at the Plymouth garrison, the King was so impressed with him that he was made a yeoman of the King's Guards and His Majesty even commissioned Sir Geoffrey Kneller, the Court artist, to paint Payne's portrait. The result was a very handsome full-length study of Payne in his ornate uniform and it can be seen now at the Museum in Truro, where it is on public exhibition. One can also purchase there a postcard reproduction of the picture.

The picture itself had a chequered history and it is fortunate that it is still surviving in such good condition. Many, many years after it was painted it was discovered by Cornish historian C.S. Gilbert at Penheale, near Launceston, a former residence of the Grenville family. When Mr Gilbert found the picture it was rolled up like a carpet, very dirty and in very poor condition and the farmer's wife living in the house gladly sold it to him for the then princely sum of £8.

After that it passed through the hands of several owners and was then put into London sale-rooms where someone recognised it as Kneller's work and it sold for £800. It next turned up among the effects of Admiral Tucker of Trematon Castle when his chattels

were sold after his death and on that occasion it was bought by Sir Robert Harvey, who presented it to the Royal Institution of Cornwall.

With the natural curiosity about mysterious passages, most people are tempted to venture through the fifteenth-century granite arches into the narrow drangway in Stratton, usually known as The Drangett. It is actually beneath as well as between two houses in the centre of the town and leads to that little haven of tranquillity, Gibraltar Square.

The name seems a bit out of place in a Cornish market town and the sight of a house named 'Gibraltar' and bearing two plaques, one inscribed 'R.S. GIBR.1785' and the other the seemingly inexplicable '12th Regt. of Foot', are bound to perplex.

Actually the answer is quite straightforward and is a delightful bit of local history which has survived to the present day. The initials 'R.S.' on the house stand for Robert Smith, a sergeant in the 12th Regiment of Foot – the Suffolk Regiment – who fought at the siege of Gibraltar in 1785 and was wounded in the action. After the relief of Gibraltar he was returned to England and was paid off at Plymouth, still in a weak state as the result of his wounds. There he made the acquaintance of a Stratton girl called Jewell, who nursed him back to health. During the process he fell in love and married Miss Jewell and as she wished to return to Stratton they decided to set up home in the town.

Robert Smith bought an old wine store and a bit of land in a courtyard at the back of some dwellings and there he demolished the store, built on the site

Taken on the occasion of Queen Victoria's Jubilee when this area was named Jubilee Square.

the house which he called 'Gibraltar' and turned the plot of waste ground into a garden. He also immortalised himself and his exploits with the plaques which today puzzle so many strangers to Stratton.

Miss Jewell knew her own mind and got what she wanted. She was typical of all Stratton folk, who have always been fiercely independent and determined to stand up for what they saw as their rights. History is peppered with their militant actions over several issues in times gone by. They took part with enthusiasm in the fifteenth-century rising led by Perkin Warbeck, who laid claim to the English throne and who at Bodmin declared himself 'king' and laid siege to Exeter with his 'Cornish army' which included many Stratton men. After this final attempt in 1496 he was captured and later hanged but Stratton supported him to the end.

Then a year later Stratton men were on the march again when they became part of the army of so-called 'rake hells' led by Michael Joseph, the St Keverne blacksmith, who marched to London in protest against taxes levied by Henry VIII to finance war with Scotland. This was another lost cause but the people of Stratton were undeterred and in 1549 they were 'against the stream' again when they were involved in strong protests against the new Prayer Book.

Then Queen Elizabeth I decreed 'the wearing of thick knitted woollen caps upon the Sabbath and Holy Days' with a fine of 3s. 4d. to be paid by anyone disobeying this ruling. The people of Stratton flatly refused to wear woollen caps because they made fine leather ones in their town which was famed for its leatherwork. They never did wear woollen caps and they were fined three times – something which might have daunted lesser mortals than Stratton folk.

In 1836 there was rebellion again in the town. The new Poor Law met the farmers' demand for the reduction of rates but it was noteworthy that the only rioting in Cornwall against the new workhouses occurred in the agricultural unions of Stratton and Camelford, where troops had to be called in to protect the Poor Law Commissioner, a Mr Gilbert, in 1837.

Stratton and Bude have not always seen eye to eye either. A hundred years ago, in March 1884, there was a great deal of controversy and some harsh words were spoken about the question of sewage in Stratton. The stream into which the drainage entered, flows into the sea at Bude and Bude people were not at all pleased about the way Stratton refused to consider an alleviation of what must have been a quite considerable nuisance. Stratton independence again!

Peter Trick in the early 1900s – he was an inmate for years of the Stratton workhouse.

Incidentally, sewage was not the only effluvium with which Stratton was at one time afflicted. It was renowned as a centre for the growing of garlic and despite the plant being very attractive to look at, the strong onion smell is not to everyone's taste.

Something connected with its inhabitants for which Stratton would have got in the record books in the past was the longevity of its residents. Elizabeth Cornish was 113 years 4 months and 15 days old when she died and was buried on 10 March 1691 in Stratton churchyard. According to a contemporary writer – maybe the local newspaper reporter of the day – she attributed her good health and long life to 'plain living, rising at sunrise, going to bed at sunset and sniffing a freshly dug turf every day'.

But even this remarkable character was outdone by her own father John Veal, who lived to be 114 years 4 months and 15 days according to an early chronicler – odd that the numbers of months and days were the same as his daughter. He put his long life down to never drinking spirituous liquors when young and when old rising at six a.m. all year round, and to never eating meat.

A man called Chamont from the same town was said to have lived to the age of 130 and have been uncle and great uncle to three hundred and sixty children! Since these people were probably illiterate one has, these days, to wonder if their counting was accurate. Perhaps it was the garlic that kept them going – there is an old Cornish saying that a person will never die while they can still smell onions.

No chapter about Stratton would be complete

The Reverend R.S. Hawker, one of North Cornwall's most colourful personalities, lived as a boy in Stratton. He was well known as the Vicar of Morwenstow.

57

Left: Hawker's hut on the cliffs at Morwenstow where he went to write. Right: A quiet scene in Stratton churchyard – Hawker's father was vicar of St Andrew's.

without mention of its connection with one of North Cornwall's most famous personalities, the Reverend R.S. Hawker, vicar of Morwenstow from 1834 to 1875. Hawker's father, the Reverend Jacob Stephen Hawker, was vicar of Stratton and the young Robert Stephen was wellknown in the town as a fun-loving youth, always planning practical jokes to surprise and amuse people.

Sadly, his father's vicarage is no more; it was long ago demolished to make way for a more modern dwelling and all that remains is the venerable fig tree which overhangs the vicarage wall – at one time a feature of the vicarage garden.

The Reverend R.S. Hawker always retained an affection for Stratton. He was immensely proud of its reputation as a town producing some of the finest cordwainers in the country and he always had his footwear made by them; he also had the saddle for his famous pony, Carrow, made by a Stratton craftsman. There were two tanneries in the town at one time and up to World War II there were still several saddlers and cordwainers in the town. The merchants who dealt in leather were among the wealthiest of the Stratton inhabitants and people came from miles around to buy leather and leather goods prepared or made in Stratton.

Over the years Stratton continued to nurture personalities in varying walks of life. One who can

Bude panorama showing its development during the early part of this century.

still be remembered by some of the oldest people in the town is Mr George Brendon, M.F.H., who lived at Broomhill. He was a great benefactor and he toiled hard and long in the interests of the people of Stratton and the promotion of the town. He helped forcefully in the negotiations which led to the bringing of a water supply to Stratton and Bude and, through his service as a county councillor, Statton district obtained the maining of so many miles of road; he also played a big part in opening up Bude as a health resort and initiated coaching for the convenience of visitors.

But first and foremost Mr Brendon is remembered as a fox-hunting man. It was his great passion in life; he claimed that he had been riding on the crupper of his father's saddle since the age of three. In his adult life he formed a pack of foxhounds, buying a pack in Ireland and adding to it a few couples from another wellknown hunting man of the day, Mr Scott-Browne, whose kennels were famous. Mr Brendon always said that his one interest was fox-hunting and that he had never caught a fish or killed a pheasant in his life.

In July 1904, when Mr Brendon had been a resident in Stratton for thirty two years, he was invited by the residents of Stratton and Bude to a dinner and entertainment and during the evening was presented with a portrait of himself in the hunting field, accompanied by his two sons, who were also keen followers to hounds. The painting, by Mr Heywood Hardy, was entitled *Drawing Cover* and was described at the time as 'a noble picture embodying a typical hunting scene'.

Contributors to the gift ranged from landowners to the poorest widow in Stratton, a measure of the affection and esteem in which Mr Brendon was held in the neighbourhood. It was said at the time that the people of Bude, who had also contributed to the gift, did not do so as generously as the people of Stratton, but then Stratton has always regarded Bude as its very much younger brother of whom it did not expect as much in any field as could be provided by Stratton.

THE BUDE CANAL

No book about Bude and Stratton would be complete without a chapter on one of the greatest although much underestimated engineering projects of its time – the Bude Canal. This remarkable construction, part of which can still be enjoyed at the Bude end, was a long time coming to fruition. It enjoyed some early prosperity and then for various reasons sank into final oblivion, although it did operate commercially for close on 70 years.

Cornishman John Edyvean put forward the suggestion for a canal from Bude to Launceston in the year 1774 and it was taken so seriously that a House of Lords Committee discussed a Bill and an Act was passed and given Royal Assent that year for a canal to be constructed, even allowing for it to be continued as far as Calstock, far beyond Launceston. But the euphoria generated by the suggestion soon died and, after all, the scheme was shelved.

In 1777, 1778, 1785 and 1793 further schemes were put forward and meetings held to assess their feasibility but still nothing really happened. Several prominent people and landed gentry of the day had ideas and plans for canals and all in all the situation was confused and somewhat explosive.

It was not until two landowners in what is now part of the parish of Bridgerule, Mr Braddon of Newacott and Mr Harward of Tackbeare, concerned about lack of employment for the men coming back from the Napoleonic Wars, enlisted the help of the then Lord Stanhope to revive the scheme for a canal, with the object of conveying the mineral-rich sand from Bude to areas where the land was poor, the sand acting as a valuable fertiliser.

After many trials and tribulations things really got under way and in 1817 the first proposed line for a canal was published. It was a very ambitious affair with the canal not only going to Launceston – with termination at Ridgegrove Mill, near the Tamar – but also with another branch going nearly to Okehampton in Devon. Almost immediately that plan ran into trouble because, for a very good reason, the Duke of Northumberland refused to allow the canal to be cut through his property in the parish of Werrington, near Launceston.

The story of how the canal finally came to be constructed is a long one and cannot be detailed here.

An aerial view of the canal, harbour and lock gate at Bude.

Mrs Emma Adams holding a portrait of her father who was a boatman on the canal.

Suffice it to say that the Bude Harbour and Canal Company was finally formed in 1819, an Act of Parliament being granted in that year for the construction of a canal to terminate three miles from Launceston, because of the Duke of Northumberland's objections, and with a main line to Holsworthy and beyond.

Work commenced in July 1819 and Lord Stanhope, prime mover in the project, travelled from his home in Kent to lay the first stone for the new breakwater

Bude canal and harbour in the late nineteenth century – the old sea captains had to exercise great skill in getting their vessels through the narrow lock entrance with sometimes only inches to spare.

'The first section of the canal to open was the Bude–Holsworthy line . . .'
Left: Burmsdon Aqueduct.
Right: Approaching Holsworthy today – it is strange to think of the town as a port.

and to cut the first turf at the spot scheduled for the canal basin. There were great celebrations on that day with banquets for honoured guests in specially erected 'pavilions' on Summerleaze Downs and for the general public free refreshments were served elsewhere on the Downs and a programme of sports arranged to entertain the estimated twelve thousand people present to witness the inauguration ceremony.

Construction work was comparatively speedy despite labour relations, technical difficulties and sometimes downright hostility from landowners and tenants through whose land the canal was to run.

The canal was finally opened for traffic, amid much rejoicing, in July 1823. The first section to open was the Bude–Holsworthy line, plus the feeder to the reservoir, to be soon followed by the Red Post to Tamerton Bridge branch. The actual opening ceremony was performed not, as might have been expected, by Lord Stanhope but by a Mr Blackmore, an Exeter businessman who was a principal shareholder in the Canal Company. The town of Holsworthy was the centre of the festivities on that day with bands playing, church bells ringing and the population, swelled by people from outlying districts, generally en fête.

The first section of the canal to Hele Bridge, Marhamchurch, was a barge canal. Left: The house of George Casebourne, the canal engineer, at Hele Bridge. Below: The Canal as it looks today between Hele Bridge and the Marhamchurch incline plane.

The Buller's Arms at Marhamchurch.

Above Hele Bridge the waterway was worked by tub boats. Here, the remains of a tub boat is displayed outside the museum at Bude.

The first section of the canal, from Bude to Hele Bridge, Marhamchurch, was a barge canal with 50 foot barges operating on it. At Hele Bridge the narrower part of the canal commenced and all the rest of the waterway was worked by tub boats only 20 feet long and 5 feet 6 inches wide as against the 13 foot of the barges.

At Hele Bridge the Canal Company built a handsome house for its engineer, overlooking the basin and even offering the facility of a reserved mooring for the canal engineer's own personal barge. At Hele Bridge there was a complex of warehouses, sawpit and stables as that was the main centre for the transferring of merchandise from the barges to the smaller tub boats.

The canal was, in effect, an amphibious railway with a series of six incline planes up and down which the tub boats travelled on rails, the boats being fitted with heavy iron wheels. The longest plane was at Hobbacott, where a complicated system of giant buckets in wells 225 feet deep backed up by an engine, which was always breaking down, hauled

A Bude Canal tub boat and old canal photographs on show in Exeter Maritime museum.

Mr W.H. Gregory of Bude with three tub boat wheels which he dredged from the canal near Rodds Bridge.

the boats up the 935 feet of the plane. The black-smith's shop, canal office and some cottages for employees were also situated at Hobbacott.

The best preserved of the incline planes today is the Werrington one, on the Red Post – Druxton branch – now part of a private residential property.

There were five aqueducts on the canal, the finest of which, at Burmsdon on the Holsworthy line, is still intact, although also on private land. The small one over the Tala Water at Bridgetown in the parish of Werrington can be seen from the public road. The aqueducts at Bridgerule, Tamerton and Tamartown, Werrington, have all been demolished; the Bridgerule one was a wooden structure.

Unfortunately, during the whole period of its existence as a working waterway the canal was plagued with misfortunes ranging from constant breakdowns of machinery, slipping banks and, in the winter, frozen stretches, to the washing away of the Bridgetown aqueduct and the almost complete destruction of Bude breakwater in storms. Added to this were what later proved to be bad management and also the conniving of traders, who conceived ingenious plans for non-payment of dues. Although in its early years the canal proved quite viable and even successful, it failed to maintain its early buoyancy as a commercial concern and the coming of the railway finally killed it off, after a long period in which it had not even been paying its way.

Ambitious early plans for continuing the line of the canal far into west Devon were soon abandoned but even so the canal operated for a period of nearly 70 years, finally closing down and being abandoned in 1891. It was a sad end to an imaginative project which started so magnificently and which many now wish was still in use.

Left: The aqueduct over the Tala Water at Bridgetown, Werrington. It replaced the original one which was washed away in the 1838 floods.

CHARACTERS FAMOUS & NOT SO FAMOUS

No visitor can fail to spot one of the most prominent buildings in Bude; the Castle, now housing local government offices and other municipal facilities. It is an impressive building created by the famous engineer and inventor Sir Goldsworthy Gurney who was born in Padstow in 1793 and practised as a doctor and surgeon in Wadebridge in his young days and later in London.

Sir Goldsworthy was particularly interested in sand, which seems a strange thing for a doctor to adopt as an absorbing passion but whilst living at Wadebridge he analysed the local sea sand and recommended its use for manure. Legend has it that he built The Castle at Bude because he wanted to prove it was possible to erect a stable building on sand. He certainly succeeded in that ambition because The Castle is as sturdy and stable today as it was on the day that it was completed.

Sir Goldsworthy invented many contrivances which contributed to the saving of life, including a miner's safety lamp and what he called the 'Bude Light' for lighthouses. He was also reputed to have driven the first ever mechanical vehicle to traverse English roads – a steam coach which he personally drove from London to Bath in 1829 at a speed of five miles per hour, an incredibly long journey for a vehicle travelling at that speed.

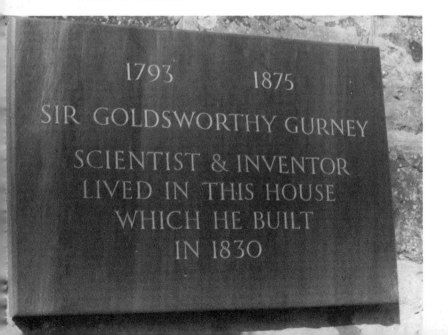

1793   1875
SIR GOLDSWORTHY GURNEY
SCIENTIST & INVENTOR
LIVED IN THIS HOUSE
WHICH HE BUILT
IN 1830

Left: Tablet placed by Bude Old Cornwall Society at The Castle, Bude (right) – built by Sir Goldsworthy Gurney.

'Legend has it that Gurney built the Castle at Bude (left) because he wanted to prove it was possible to erect a stable building on sand.' Below: Nanny Moore's Bridge and the Castle in the background.

Bude, Old Bridge and Castle

Sir Goldsworthy died at Reeds, Poughill, in 1875 at the age of 82 and an inscription below the clock in the tower there, given by his daughter in memory of her father, states that 'his Inventions and Discoveries in Steam and Electricity made Communication by Land and Sea so rapid that it became necessary for all England to keep Uniform Clock time'. What an epitaph. Incidentally, when Sir Goldsworthy's will was proved in 1875 he left less than £300 but in 1980 his home, Reeds, was on the market with an asking price of £90,000.

Like most places, Bude has had its fair share of 'characters' over the years but a book published in 1984 dealing with the exploits of Captain Shaw, a former chief of the London Fire Brigade, shed light upon an extraordinary person, one Samuel Seccombe by name, who lived at Burgoyne Cottages, Bude in 1871 with his wife and four children. Apparently Samuel had been a tallyman draper, travelling around and selling drapery items from door to door in the method which forestalled the modern mail order catalogue.

In 1871 Samuel Seccombe left Bude and went to London – to lead a remarkably crooked life as a charity collector. Not that charity collectors were crooked, it was just that Samuel had hit upon an idea for turning good work to his own very questionable benefit: spending the money given to him by generous benefactors to aid the cause for which he was collecting and even inventing a few charities of his own on the side, favouring particularly those which purported to be relieving distress among injured firemen or had other connections with the then London Fire Brigade. This extraordinary state of

Ebbingford Manor (right), one of the finest houses in the area, is today privately owned. For the whole of the thirteenth century it was part of the royal Duchy of Cornwall. Later it became the property of the famous Arundel family and later still was inherited by Sir Thomas Acland. After the building of St Michael & All Angels' Church, Sir Thomas generously bequeathed Ebbingford to the Church Commissioners as a vicarage. Then in 1953 the vicar, Canon Walter Prest, who was priest at Bude from 1944 until 1970, came to an arrangement with his friend Sir Dudley Stamp CBE to exchange houses; Sir Dudley was then living nearby at Falcon Terrace. The present owner is Mr Brian Dudley Stamp.

affairs went on for thirty years until Seccombe was 80 years of age and said to have been making a very appreciable income from his nefarious doings.

Although brought before the court on a number of occasions and serving several short prison sentences Seccombe's 'occupation' was so profitable that it made all these minor irritations quite insignificant to him. Fortunately for Bude he does not appear to have returned to his native town – presumably the pickings to be gleaned from his 'charity work' were much more lucrative in the London area. Even so there were those in the Cornish town who had welcomed his visits with his stock as a tallyman and for that reason missed him when he left.

Left: The path to the beach – looking back to the river and the town of Bude. Again Herbert Hughes captures the scene – this time in 1913.

FUN AND FROLIC

Long before it became a popular holiday resort Bude had plenty of attractions to entertain both its residents and those who came from neighbouring areas.

We have already seen how lifeboat practice was a popular spectator 'sport' in days gone by but on a less serious note was the annual Bude Fair which attracted hundreds of people to the town. This was a cattle fair as well as being an amusement venue. The wellknown Westcountry showman family of Hancock regularly attended the event and set up their whirligigs and other rides on the lower marsh opposite The Crescent, while on the other side of Bude the cheapjacks, quack doctors and purveyors of all kinds of goods arranged their stalls.

Heavily laden excursion trains brought in crowds of people and others travelled miles on foot, horseback and by horse and cart and horse and carriage to attend the Fair. All manner of goods were on sale from baskets to fruit, from clothing to fish.

The cattle sale was the serious side of the event. An idea of the atmosphere of this day of all days in the Bude calendar can be gleaned from a report in the *Launceston Weekly News* of 28 September 1861 which says: 'Bude Fair on Monday last was well attended by those interested in the sale and purchase of cattle but business was generally dull. The pleasure department of the Fair was in lively mood. Young people in large numbers crowded the rather confined area of the proceedings while owners of standing seemed to be doing a brisk trade in their attractive confectionery.'

A rather amusing occurrence at the same Fair was reported, although it was probably not funny at the time to those affected by it! Today we can smile at the serious newspaper paragraph that tells us that at the 1861 Fair 'an occasional shower of tropical violence came with damaging and detracting effect on the fair wearers of crinoline. At times the lightning accompanying the storm was very vivid and caused some ladies to adopt the precautionary measure of withdrawing the steel from their balloon-like dresses'. The sight of lots of ladies dismantling their crinolines must have been vastly entertaining!

Bude still gets its fun fair and rides which these days are erected on the Wharf and attract plenty of people from miles around, but the old-style Fair died out long ago and cattle are never seen in the streets of Bude these days.

Modern fun and frolic centres more on water

Bude Fair being held on The Strand at the turn of the century.

Fair Day in Bude in the nineteenth century.

Water sports on the canal at Bude in the early 1900s.

Grandstand view at Bude swimming gala . . .

. . . the swimming pool has been constructed under the cliffs on the northern side of Bude beach.

Bude picture house.

sports. Bude has developed into a popular centre for surfers and the breakers which roll in from the Atlantic are often many feet high. However, if surf is fun it can also be dangerous and Bude can boast of having the first surf life-saving club to be formed in Britain – way back in 1953. In 1980 the Duke of Edinburgh, Patron of the Surf Life-Saving Association of Great Britain, presented Certificates of Merit, the Association's highest award, to the crew of the Bude Surf Life-Saving Club who went to the aid of a catamaran in difficulty off Bude the previous year. The Surf Life-Saving Club is one of the most active organisations in the town, attracting a steady stream of young people. Club stalwarts Jonathon Ball, Peter Cloke, Tim Higham, Mike Moyle and Peter Vickery all received long-service awards in 1984 during a visit by a team from the New South Wales State Life-Saving Association in Australia, whose chairman, incidentally, said at the time that surf conditions at Bude were comparable to those in New South Wales.

The Bude Canal has left the area with another popular recreational venue – Tamar Lake. In 1820 what has now become the Lower Lake was built between Kilkhampton and Bradworthy as the feeder reservoir for the Bude Canal. It was a major engineering feat of its day and it served the canal well. When the canal ceased to function Tamar Lake was left to be claimed by nature but it was later brought into service to supply piped water to the Bude area and served this purpose for over 70 years.

In 1978, with the march of progress, the new Upper Lake was constructed as a reservoir and the original Tamar Lake was handed back to nature again and it is now a delightful recreational area, a wildlife and bird sanctuary and a very popular venue for those interested in coarse fishing, as it contains bream, carp, rudd and tench and has no close season, so anglers can be seen on its banks all year round.

The Upper Lake offers sailing, boardsailing and canoeing as well as fly fishing for rainbow trout with which it has been stocked by the South West Water Authority. What a difference from the days when tub boats used to unload or take on goods at Virworthy Wharf, the terminal point for traffic on the feeder arm of the Bude Canal.

The feeder arm itself, which runs through some of the most remote and wild country in Devon, still meanders along a line that can for the most part be clearly followed. During the days when it was used

The 3rd Battalion of the Devon and Cornwall Light Infantry entering Bude.

for the Bude water supply it retained much the appearance that it had when it was part of a working canal system.

Now it is choked solid with wild vegetation, most of it horsetails, that strange plant which is a throw-back to prehistoric times. It flourishes in the dried-up bed of the canal feeder arm as it surely flourishes nowhere else, so tall, thick and dense are its stems. Where it is not choked out by horsetail the 'flag', the wild yellow iris, creates a beautiful splash of colour in its flowering season. Even in its demise the feeder arm of the Bude Canal is poignantly beautiful; undisturbed nature has taken over where man left off and has proved that she always holds the trump hand in the end.

Incidentally, during World War II Bude was not the sleepy, cut-off-from-reality seaside town that some people may have imagined it was. Although the subject hardly comes under the terms of 'Fun and Frolic' this seems a good place to mention it because there was a lot of pleasure generated even during those grim times. During the war Bude played host to the crack American Commando unit, the Second Rangers Batallion of the US Army, which trained on the formidable cliffs of the North Cornish coast.

The Americans mingled well with the people of Bude and many lasting friendships were cemented. In 1984, forty years after D-Day, a group of those Rangers who were billeted in the town in 1943–44 returned to renew acquaintance with old friends. The visit came about because former US Army Sergeant, Tommy Ruggiero, found among his late mother's possessions the address of the Marshall family, with whom he had been billeted during the war years. On their return the Rangers were fêted with the same hospitality that they had known forty years before: a tree, presented by Bude–Stratton town council was planted in the Shute Triangle in the centre of the town to commemorate 'the close links between the Second Rangers Battalion US Army and the town in 1943–44'. The tree also commemorates Ranger friends and colleagues who did not return from the war.

Captain Ralph Goranson, formerly with C Company of the 2nd Rangers, then presented a plaque to the town, to thank their hosts and all the people of Bude for the hospitality given to the Rangers. There was laughter and tears and a thoroughly happy day spent by all, including a tour by the Rangers of the North Cornish coast and the cliffs they knew so well. A happy note on which to end.

Right: Looking toward Widemouth.

ACKNOWLEDGMENTS

My grateful thanks to all who have helped me with the compilation of this little volume – all those who lent old photographs for reproduction – acknowledged on another page – and also Mr F. Daniel, *The Cornish & Devon Post*, *The Western Morning News*, Cornwall County Library Services Launceston Branch, the late Mrs B. Worden and the Cornwall Buildings Preservation Trust.

Werrington, Launceston, 1984.   Joan Rendell

PLATE ACKNOWLEDGMENTS

Front cover colouring by Paul Honeywill
Michael Smith: pages 4, 5, 10, 11, 13, 25–7, 40, 63
R. Spencer Thorn: pages 8, 12, 17, 18, 29, 57, 60, 70, 81, 88–91
Ray Bishop: pages 37, 41, 44–7, 51, 52, 59, 77, 78
The Author: pages 6, 42, 43, 48, 53, 58, 64, 66–9, 71–6
Royal Institution of Cornwall: pages 9, 18–21, 30, 33, 35, 36, 38, 39, 49, 50, 82, 93
Mrs H. Ellacott: pages 15, 23, 34, 65, 85, 87
Mrs E. Boundy: pages 24, 86
Jack Bickle: pages 16, 28
The late Mrs B. Worden: pages 55, 56
David Clarke: page 3
Mike Miller: page 7
Mrs Nosworthy: page 14
Joan Madge: page 22
J. McLeod: page 79

NORTH CORNWALL IN THE OLD DAYS

by Joan Rendell, 147 old photographs.

These pictures and Joan Rendell's perceptive text combine to give us many facets of a nostalgic way of North Cornish life, stretching from Newquay to the Cornwall/Devon border.

'This remarkable collection of pictures is a testimony to a people, a brave and uncomplaining race.'

Pamela Leeds, The Western Evening Herald

GATEWAY TO CORNWALL

by Joan Rendell, 72 photographs.

Joan Rendell writes about Launceston and District – a highly personal portrait of the place, some of its past and people. 'I have attempted to make this book different from other publications about the area . . .'

'A delight to lovers of the local scene and its historic background.'

Arthur Venning, The Editor,
Cornish & Devon Post

CORNISH CHURCHES

by Joan Rendell. 60 photographs and drawings.

Here in her fifth title for Bossiney Joan Rendell explores many of Cornwall's lovely churches. Music and myths, art and architecture, personalities past and present are only some of the facets of her journey across the Cornish landscape.

'. . . an author who is well qualified to take us on a tour of Cornish Churches . . . extremely readable.'

Cornish Guardian

THE CORNISH COUNTRYSIDE

by Sarah Foot. 130 illustrations, 40 in colour.

Here, in Bossiney's first colour publication, Sarah Foot explores inland Cornwall, the moors and the valleys, and meets those who work on the land.

'Sarah Foot sets out to share her obvious passion for Cornwall and to describe its enigmas . . . It is a book for those who are already in love with Cornwall and for those who would like to know her better.'

Alison Foster, The Cornish Times

VIEWS OF OLD CORNWALL

by Sarah Foot.

Nearly 200 old picture postcards from the Peter Dryden collection, with text by Sarah Foot, all combine to recall Cornwall as she once was.

'. . . will be certain to start the talk flowing of days gone by.'

The Cornishman

RIVERS OF CORNWALL

by Sarah Foot. 130 photographs, 45 in colour.

The author explores six great Cornish rivers: the Helford, the Fal, the Fowey, the Camel, the Lynher and the Tamar.

'. . . makes use of many colour illustrations as well as black and white and shows that whatever changes may have taken place in the river economics they remain places of quality and beauty, quintessentially Cornwall.'

The Cornish Guardian

SEA STORIES OF CORNWALL

by Ken Duxbury. 48 photographs.

'This is a tapestry of true tales', writes the author, 'by no means all of them disasters – which portray something of the spirit, the humour, the tragedy, and the enchantment, that is the lot of we who know the sea.'

'Ken is a sailor, and these stories are written with a close understanding and feel for the incidents.'

James Mildren, The Western Morning News

DISCOVERING BODMIN MOOR

by E. V. Thompson. 45 photographs and map.

E. V. Thompson, author of the bestselling novel, *Chase the Wind*, set on the eastern slopes of Bodmin Moor, explores the Moor past and present.

'. . . shows the moor in all its aspects – beautiful, harsh, romantic and almost cruel . . . how well he knows the character of the moor.'

The Editor, Cornish Guardian

SUPERSTITION AND FOLKLORE

by Michael Williams. 45 photographs.

Romany reflections, old country customs, interviews and superstitious people, folklore from both Devon and Cornwall, omens and coincidences are all featured.

'. . . has all the ingredients of a mini-bestseller.'

Cornwall Courier

VIEWS OF OLD DEVON

Rosemary Anne Lauder provides the text for more than 200 old postcards, evocative of a world and a way of life that has gone. Words and pictures combine to produce a book that will delight all who love Devon.

'Only the camera can turn back the clock like this.'

The Sunday Independent

VIEWS OF OLD PLYMOUTH

by Sarah Foot.
Words and old pictures combine to recall Plymouth as it once was: a reminder of those great times past and of the spirit of the people of Plymouth.
'This is a lovely nostalgia-ridden book and one which no real Plymothian will want to be without.'
James Mildren, The Western Morning News

VIEWS OF OLD EXMOOR

by Rosemary Anne Lauder.
Words and 140 old photographs combine to take us back in mood and time . . . a book destined to delight all who love Exmoor.
' . . . will provide a passport for many trips down memory lane . . .'
The Bideford Gazette

LEGENDS OF SOMERSET

by Sally Jones. 65 photographs and drawings.
Sally Jones travels across rich legendary landscapes. Words, drawings and photographs all combine to evoke a spirit of adventure.
'On the misty lands of the Somerset Plain – as Sally Jones makes clear – history, legend and fantasy are inextricably mixed.'
Dan Lees, The Western Daily Press

SOMERSET IN THE OLD DAYS

by David Young. 145 old photographs.
David Young of TSW takes a journey in words and old pictures across Somerset.

STRANGE SOMERSET STORIES

Introduced by David Foot with chapters by Ray Waddon, Jack Hurley, Lornie Leete-Hodge, Hilary Wreford, David Foot, Rosemary Clinch and Michael Williams.
' . . . a good collection of yarns about Somerset's eccentrics, weird legends and architectural follies . . .'
Dan Lees, The Western Daily Press

100 YEARS ON BODMIN MOOR

by E. V. Thompson. 145 photographs.
A rich harvest of old photographs and picture post-cards, reflecting life on the Moor for a century with perceptive text.
' . . . timely that such a publication and collection of photographs should appear now, as a record for all of those who have loved and been inspired by Bodmin Moor.'
Sarah Foot, The Western Morning News

DARTMOOR IN THE OLD DAYS

by James Mildren. 145 photographs.
James Mildren is an author who is at home in the wilderness of his Dartmoor.
'Lovers of Dartmoor will need no persuasion to obtain a copy. To anybody else, I suggest they give it a try. It may lead to a better understanding of why many people want Dartmoor to remain a wonderful wilderness.'
Keith Whitfort, The Western Evening Herald

SEA STORIES OF DEVON

In this companion volume to *Sea Stories of Cornwall* nine Westcountry authors recall stirring events and people from Devon's sea past. Well illustrated with old and new photographs, it is introduced by best-selling novelist E. V. Thompson.
'The tales themselves are interesting and varied but the real strength of the book lies in the wealth of illustration, with photographs and pictures on practically every page.'
Jane Leigh, Express & Echo

UNKNOWN DEVON

by Rosemary Anne Lauder, Monica Wyatt and Michael Williams. 73 illustrations.
In Unknown Devon three writers explore off-the-beaten track places in Devon.
'If you want to extend your knowledge of hidden Devon then this well-illustrated book is a handy companion.'
Mid-Devon Advertiser

We shall be pleased to send you our catalogue giving full details of our growing list of titles for Devon, Cornwall and Somerset and forthcoming publications.

If you have difficulty in obtaining our titles, write direct to Bossiney Books, Land's End, St Teath, Bodmin, Cornwall.